THE MISSING IGUANA MYSTERY

by Andy Tang

illustrated by Nicole Wong

Scott Foresman
is an imprint of

PEARSON

Glenview, Illinois • Boston, Massachusetts • Chandler, Arizona
Upper Saddle River, New Jersey

Saturday afternoon I visited my friend Shirley Hong at her house on Baker Street. I went to the door and rang the bell for Shirley's family's second-floor home. After a short wait, I could hear footsteps pounding down the stairs.

"Hi, Jacob! Glad you could come over," Shirley said. She turned around, and I followed her back upstairs.

Allow me to introduce myself. My name is Jacob Wilson, and, together with my friend Shirley Hong, I solve mysteries.

"Did you bring your 'Mystery Mansion' video game?" Shirley asked with a hopeful look.

"Yes, and the *Guide to Becoming a Super Sleuth* too," I replied.

"Hmm . . . let me give my sleuthing skills a try," said Shirley. She focused her attention on my appearance, and she looked me up and down intently. "I would say that you had hot dogs for lunch, and you took a shortcut through the playground on the way here."

Puzzled by her quick response, I asked, "How did you know that, Shirley?"

"Simple. You have a mustard stain on your collar and mud on your sneakers, which I'm happy you took off before you came in. The only place where there are still puddles after yesterday's rain is by the swing sets on the playground. Now, let's play 'Mystery Mansion'!"

Amazed, I handed her the video game, and, just as she was about to turn on the gamemaster console, the doorbell rang.

Shirley ran down the stairs and answered the door. Just as I started flipping through the super sleuthing guide, I heard her coming back up the stairs, followed by a heavier set of footsteps.

"Jacob, I think you know Pablo Rodriguez from math class," Shirley said.

Shirley went on to explain, "Pablo just told me he has a case for us. I think you'll be interested." She then turned toward our classmate and gestured. "Go ahead, Pablo."

"My pet iguana is missing," Pablo began. "When I peeked in his cage this morning, he wasn't there. I searched everywhere for him. I'm stumped. If I don't find him, my parents are going to be upset with me. I really need your help."

"An iguana? Isn't that something like a salamander?" I asked, remembering one in an exhibit at the Natural History Museum.

"Iguanas are reptiles, and salamanders are amphibians," Pablo noted. "Reptiles have dry, scaly skin and lay their eggs on land while amphibians have moist skin. Most amphibians lay their eggs in the water."

"Iguanas are ectotherms, which means they absorb heat from their surroundings, and they are a type of lizard. Lizards are a suborder of reptiles," Shirley added.

"Right," I said in stunned agreement. I gulped. I wanted to help Pablo, but I wasn't sure about encountering an iguana!

"Come on, let's look at the scene of the crime, shall we?" Shirley asked. The three of us walked to Pablo's house.

Once inside we greeted Pablo's dad, who was furiously typing away on his computer. Pablo explained that his dad had a deadline to meet for a newsletter. We then climbed the stairs to the attic, where Pablo kept his iguana's cage.

"This is where I keep Ziggy, my iguana," Pablo explained.

Ziggy's cage was larger than I had expected, standing four feet tall, extending six feet long, and three feet wide. I shuddered at the thought of Ziggy being as big as a German shepherd.

Pablo seemed to sense my concern and said, "Iguanas like to climb trees when they're in the wild, so they need the room. Don't worry. Ziggy is still a baby, so he's not very big."

I let out a sigh of relief. Meanwhile, Shirley was looking into the cage and around the attic for clues. The cage was made of metal wire and had a wooden frame. Inside there were branches of different heights—one reached the top of the cage. There were also a few shelves for Ziggy to lie on to bask in the glow of the heat lamps that Pablo has to keep him warm. A plate heaping with his favorite greens sat in the corner of the cage. The side that faced the stairs also had a door through which Pablo could let Ziggy out or clean his cage.

"When was the last time you saw Ziggy?" Shirley asked Pablo.

"Last night, when I checked on him before I went to bed," replied Pablo.

"Are you the only one who takes care of Ziggy?" Shirley asked.

"Yes," Pablo replied. "The conditions my parents set for me having Ziggy were that I would be responsible for feeding him, cleaning up, and paying for Ziggy's veterinarian bills by doing odd jobs around the house."

"Who else is in your family?" Shirley quizzed.

"My father, whom you saw downstairs, and my mother, who is a nurse, but she's working late and won't be home until this evening. I also have a little brother, Juan, who's seven, and he's around somewhere," explained Pablo.

"Well," said Shirley, "I think I've seen enough here. Let's go interview the rest of your family, Pablo."

Pablo nodded and we descended the stairs from the attic. We walked into the den where Pablo's father was taking a break from his typing.

"Excuse me, Mr. Rodriguez," Shirley said, "I'm Shirley Hong and this is Jacob Wilson," nodding in my direction. "We're trying to locate Ziggy, so may I ask when you saw him last?"

Mr. Rodriguez looked up at Shirley as if baffled by the question and replied, "I haven't seen him recently." He scratched his head. "I've been so busy with work lately. Pablo, you've been keeping him in his cage, haven't you?"

Pablo hesitated and drew in a deep breath, but his father had already turned back to the computer and did not notice him nod his head *yes*. Pablo raised his eyebrows as though he were about to add something, but Shirley cut in. "Thank you, Mr. Rodriguez," she said.

"I'm sorry—I'm preoccupied with finishing this newsletter," said Mr. Rodriguez without looking at Shirley. "As soon as I complete it, I'll be able to answer more questions if you need me to." He then began reading the text on his computer screen out loud. Shirley looked at Pablo and me.

"Let's go look for Juan," Shirley said.

"Do you think Pablo's father knows where Ziggy might be?" I asked as we walked into the hallway.

"No," Shirley said with confidence. "I think he is too busy with work to notice." Pablo nodded in agreement.

After following Pablo through various parts of the house, we found Juan in his room. Pablo knocked gently on the door and asked if we could enter. We heard a sniffle and a quiet *yes.*

"Are you OK?" said Pablo when we entered Juan's room. Juan shrugged as he quickly wiped his eyes. Pablo introduced us as his friends who were there to help him locate Ziggy.

"Am I in trouble?" Juan asked anxiously.

"No, no, Juan, we're just trying to find Ziggy. You haven't seen him have you?" Pablo said.

"Just yesterday, when I watched you take him out of his cage for exercise," Juan replied without looking directly at his brother.

"Juan, do you like Ziggy?" questioned Shirley.

"Oh yes, very much," Juan replied.

"Pablo," Shirley said as she turned to him, "do you let Juan share the responsibilities of caring for Ziggy?"

"Well, no," answered Pablo. "When I first got Ziggy, my parents said that I was responsible for everything involving him. Why do you ask?"

"Well, maybe Juan has something to share with us about Ziggy. How about it, Juan?" Shirley gently prodded.

"Actually, I did see Ziggy this morning," Juan explained. "Pablo was still asleep, and I wanted to say 'good morning' to Ziggy. When I went up to the attic, he seemed excited to see me, and he clawed at the sides of his cage. I thought it would be OK to let him out for a little while, but when I opened the cage door, Ziggy ran out really fast. I looked around but I couldn't find him, so I closed the cage door and went to my room. I hope you're not mad at me, Pablo."

Pablo did not say anything for a while. Then he spoke slowly. "Of course I'm not mad at you, Juan. I just wish you had told me about it earlier this morning."

"Well, now that we have that cleared up, it looks like Ziggy is just lost and not stolen or kidnapped," I cheerily pointed out. "Right, Shirley?"

"That is correct," declared Shirley. "Pablo, you said you looked all over the house for Ziggy, but I have a strong suspicion that Ziggy is still somewhere in the house. Pablo, you and Juan should start looking downstairs and work your way up. Jacob and I will start from Ziggy's cage in the attic and work our way down. Does that sound like a plan to everyone?"

The three of us nodded our heads in agreement.

"Good," Shirley said. "Let's get started."

When we arrived once again in the attic, Shirley began looking at the walls and corners with a magnifying glass.

"What on Earth could you find there?" I asked impatiently.

"Claw marks," Shirley replied knowingly.

"You don't think Ziggy scaled the attic walls in order to escape, do you?" I joked.

Shirley kept examining and inspecting as she roamed the attic. She spied a skylight at the end nearest the stairs and examined it as well.

"Do you suppose Ziggy planned to take flying lessons once he opened the skylight?" I teased.

"No, I'm afraid not," Shirley answered plainly. "You see this crank here? It needs to be turned to open up the skylight, and Ziggy would have a lot of trouble getting through here. Come on, let's go back downstairs."

I threw my arms up in exasperation as I followed Shirley out of the attic. She sure knew a lot about solving mysteries!

When we got downstairs Shirley faced me and said, "I'll check the rooms while you check the closets in the hallway, OK?"

"Fine," I mumbled. I was thinking that I had better pay closer attention to clues if I wanted to be as good a detective as Shirley.

I approached the first closet down the hall, imagining Ziggy jumping down from the top shelf and landing on my head with his dry, scaly tail grazing my neck. I shivered as I slowly turned the knob and opened the closet door. Whew! It was only a linen closet full of sheets and towels.

The next one should be easy, I thought. I grabbed the knob and swung open the door.

A small winged creature flew straight into my face. I slapped furiously around my face and head, sputtering, because I felt like it flew into my mouth. I patted down my clothes and wiped my sleeve across my face. What was that, I worried, as I looked up at the ceiling? There by the hallway light fluttered a large gray moth.

I let out a sigh of relief—it was only a moth! "Jacob, when you're done swatting at moths, would you join me for a moment?" asked Shirley.

After calming myself down, I approached the doorway where Shirley stood.

"When we go into this room, you just might be able to see where our runaway friend is," said Shirley with confidence. She stepped cautiously into the room and pointed up.

There on the top shelf of a bookcase sat Ziggy. He looked at us and bobbed his head. There were several books on the floor, probably knocked over in his climb. Sunlight streamed in from the windows and lit the entire wall where the bookcase stood.

"Why don't you go find Pablo and Juan? You can tell them the mystery has been solved, and we found their friend," Shirley suggested.

Relieved not to be on lizard guard duty, I found Pablo and Juan in the kitchen and relayed the news of Shirley's discovery. Like a stampede, the three of us ran back to the room where Shirley and Ziggy were waiting.

"Ziggy!" exclaimed Pablo and Juan. Juan jumped up and down in excitement, while Pablo's eyes beamed, and he flashed a wide smile.

Pablo dragged a stool over to the bookcase, carefully climbed onto the stool, and gently pulled Ziggy from his perch. The lizard slowly opened and closed his mouth as if to protest, but Pablo marched up to the attic to put him back in his cage. He was still grinning when he returned.

Pablo asked Shirley how she knew where to find Ziggy.

"I didn't at first," Shirley confessed, "but after examining a few things, I had a good idea of where to start looking. When you told us that Ziggy was a climber, I knew I had to look somewhere high where Ziggy could have climbed. Because of the heat lamps you have by his cage and because iguanas are ectotherms, I knew he would head for a warm place. Then Jacob and I reexamined the attic, and I saw the closed skylight. That told me that Ziggy still had to be inside the house. So, if he wasn't in the attic, Ziggy had to go to another level, even if it was downstairs. With all that warm sunlight pouring in and a nice bookcase to climb, this room fit two of Ziggy's requirements."

"This is my dad's study, and those are his reference books," Pablo said pointing to the floor. "We'd better clean up the mess!" Shirley and I nodded in agreement.

After picking up the books, Pablo thanked us and promised to let Juan share more of the responsibilities of taking care of Ziggy.

When we returned to Shirley's house, she immediately began to play "Mystery Mansion." I was still puzzled by Shirley's ability to piece together the clues that led to Ziggy's discovery.

"You know a lot about iguanas but not everything, and yet you still found Ziggy. How did you do it?" I asked her.

"You know that *Guide to Becoming a Super Sleuth* that you brought over?" she said, her face intent on the game.

"Yes," I said.

"I've already read it!"

Iguanas and Their Habitat

The common iguana is a tree-dwelling, plant-eating lizard found in the tropical regions of Mexico and South America. It can grow up to six feet long, with the tail making up about half of its length. It is usually bright green with a dark-striped tail.

Iguanas kept as pets must have heat and proper lighting in order to stay healthy. Iguanas do not make their own heat. They absorb heat from their surroundings. Their internal body temperature should be a nice warm 88°F for much of the day. Because iguanas in the wild like to bask in sunlight, light bulbs that provide a wide range of ultraviolet light are best for pet iguanas.

As iguanas grow, they like to climb, so putting some branches in their cages provides them with something on which to climb. Surfaces such as shelves also provide iguanas with places to sit or bask.